I0558009

A Shattered Heart In The Master's Hand

Overcoming Grief

Rhonda Bordes M.A., B.C.C.C.

Copyright © 2025 Rhonda Bordes
All rights reserved.

This is a work of non-fiction. Some names and identifying details may have been changed to protect the privacy of individuals.

No part of this publication, *A. Shattered Heart in the Master's Hand,* may be reproduced, stored in a retrieval system, or transmitted in any form or by any means—electronic, mechanical, photocopying, recording, or otherwise—without the prior written permission of the author, except for brief quotations used in reviews or scholarly works.

Scripture quotations marked (NIV) are taken from the Holy Bible, New International Version®, NIV®. Copyright © 1973, 1978, 1984, 2011 by Biblica, Inc.™ Used by permission of Zondervan. All rights reserved worldwide. www.zondervan.comThe "NIV" and "New International Version" are trademarks registered in the United States Patent and Trademark Office by Biblica, Inc.™

ISBN: 979-8-89778-880-4

Printed in the United States of America
First Edition, 2025

For permissions or inquiries, contact:
rhonda@evcounseling.org

DEDICATION

Son, when I was in the bowels of depression, the Lord sent you! You lifted my spirits and caused me to want to live again and now, I dedicate this book to you because throughout your life, I have witnessed your courageous journey through grief and remained too long in depression — the loss of your father, grandparents, uncles, and dear friends have marked your path. Though the weight of sorrow has often been heavy and the emotional terrain difficult to navigate, you have continued to press forward with strength and determination in pursuit of healing and freedom. I want you to know how deeply I love you and how immeasurably proud I am of the man you are becoming. May God do for you, what he sent you to do for me. It is an honor to call you my son. I love you James.

In memory of my best friend who became my sister, Ishawnta "Candi" Morrison. Words will never relay our teen-queen bond and how we looked after and defended one another. Until we meet again, I love you sissy, you are deeply missed.

CONTENTS

INTRODUCTION

Grief has been the inescapable experience of mankind - from the times of Adam and Eve until now, everyone has walked this path. Some were prophets, others were kings, mothers, sons, disciples, siblings and friends, no matter what the relationship, status, or position, each carried their own heartbreak—death, betrayal, failure, and shattered dreams.

It is a universal experience that has touched the lives of individuals since the beginning of humanity. Throughout the pages of Scripture, we see men and women who walked closely with God endure profound losses—of children, spouses, property, inheritance, friendships, and stability. Yet, in their moments of despair, God never abandoned them. Instead, He met them in their pain, offering comfort, redemption, and restoration. From David mourning his child (2 Samuel 12:15-23) to Job losing everything and later receiving double his portion Job 42:10-12), the Bible repeatedly affirms that suffering is not the end of the story. Jacob grieved for Joseph (Genesis 37:31-35), but later embraced his son in Egypt (Genesis 45:4-7). Naomi, once bitter and empty (Ruth 1:19-21), found joy in the birth of her grandson, who became part of the lineage of Christ (Ruth 4:14-15). Even the loss of friendships and relationships, as seen in David's grief over Jonathan (2 Samuel 1:25-27) or Paul's abandonment by fellow believers (2 Timothy 4:9-10), was met with divine comfort and purpose.

The lives of those in Scripture serve as a beacon of hope, proving that there is life beyond lost. David, Job, Naomi, and even the Prodigal Son all walked through deep valleys of sorrow but emerged into seasons of renewal. The same God who restored them is still at work today. Your loss does not disqualify you from God's purpose. Instead, it may be the very thing that refines you, strengthens you, and prepares you for something greater. Romans 8:28 assures us that God works all things together—even loss—for the good of those who love Him so, step forward in faith because your story is not over. God's restoration awaits. Keep walking, keep trusting, and know that joy comes in the morning (Psalm 30:5). Your best days are still ahead.

CHAPTER ONE

The Response

Grief is a natural response to loss, but its impact can be as unique as the individuals experiencing it. It is not just about mourning the death of a loved one—it can stem from the loss of a relationship, a dream, freedom, health, pets, property, a job, stability, or even identity. The weight of grief can feel overwhelming, altering your emotions, thoughts, and even your faith. In moments of profound sorrow, it is easy to wonder: Where is God in my pain? How do I move forward when what I knew or loved has changed?

While grief is often described as a process, it is important to understand that it is not a straight, predictable road with a clear beginning, middle, and end. It is a personal journey, unique to every individual. Grief does not follow a neat timeline or respond to logic; rather, it ebbs and flows like waves—sometimes crashing without warning, other times receding quietly. There are days when it feels like progress is being made, only to be followed by moments of emotional setback. It may involve circling back to old memories, pausing in numbness, or finding oneself suddenly moved forward by a moment of hope or joy. And all of it is valid. All of it is part of the human experience.

Even those in Scripture who walked intimately with God were not spared from griefs piercing touch. David wept bitterly for his sons, Job sat in ashes mourning the loss of his children and possessions, Hannah poured out her soul in anguish over infertility, and Peter wept at the remembrance of Jesus's words as the cock crowed the third time. Their stories serve as a testament to the truth that grief is not a sign of weakness or a lack of faith, but rather a natural response to love that has been disrupted by loss.

Yet in the midst of their suffering, a common thread emerges—**God did not abandon them.** He was present in their pain, patient in their questions, and faithful in their healing. In every tear, God was near. His presence was not withdrawn in their sorrow; rather, He drew closer still. He offered comfort that no human words could provide, healing that reached into the deepest wounds, and restoration that brought beauty out of ashes. This same God walks with us today. He is not distant from our sorrow; He enters it with us. He collects our tears in His bottle (Psalm 56:8), promises to give us a garment of praise instead of a spirit of despair (Isaiah 61:3), and invites us to cast all our burdens upon Him because He cares deeply for us (1 Peter 5:7). While grief may feel isolating, we are never alone. The path may be uncertain, but His companionship is sure.

Grief may change us, but it does not diminish the truth that we are still held, still loved, and still being led forward by the Shepherd of our souls.

There is Life After Loss

One of the greatest challenges of grief is believing that life can continue beyond pain. Loss can feel like the end of a chapter, leaving us uncertain about what comes next. But the Bible reassures us that God is a God of restoration. Isaiah 61:3 (NIV) declares that He gives "a crown of beauty instead of ashes, the oil of joy instead of mourning, and a garment of praise instead of a spirit of despair (heaviness)."

If you are walking through grief, know this: You are not alone. Your pain is real, but it is not permanent. Psalm 30:5 assures us that "weeping may endure for the night, but joy comes in the morning."

The seven stages of grief provide a framework to help us understand the emotional and psychological shifts that occur during loss. These stages include shock and denial, pain and guilt, anger and bargaining, depression, the upward turn, reconstruction and working through, and acceptance. While not everyone will experience every stage in the same order—or at all—this model can serve as a guide to help recognize where you are in your healing journey.

CHAPTER TWO

The Reality Of Grief: A Wound Or A Scar?

I have often wondered why the creator of *Charlie Thrown* chose the phrase *"Good Grief."* Perhaps it was meant to be irony, because in reality, there is nothing that feels good about grief. It is raw, painful, and often overwhelming. It disrupts life as we know it, forcing us to face the reality of loss in a way we never wanted or planned for. If we had our way, we would never have to experience grief again, and one day, for those who belong to Jesus, that will be our reality as the Bible promises that in eternity, there will be no more sorrow, no more pain, no more tears (Revelation 21:4). But while we are earthbound, grief is an unavoidable part of our experience. Loss is woven into the fabric of life—whether through the death of a loved one, the end of a relationship, the loss of a dream, or any significant change that alters our reality, and while grief produces pain, it's not a period but it can cause a pause in our life as we know it.

How Grief Affects Us Differently

The way we process grief is shaped by various factors, including our upbringing, cultural background, spiritual beliefs, personal resilience, and support system. Some may outwardly express their pain, while others internalize it. One person may seem to ''move on" quickly, while another may struggle with deep sorrow for years. No two people will grieve in exactly the same way, and that is okay. However, the key to healthy grieving is allowing yourself to go through the process rather than getting stuck in it.

Recognizing When You Are Stuck

While grief has no strict timeline, it is possible to remain in a particular stage for too long, causing emotional, mental, and even physical stagnation. Signs that you may be stuck in grief include:

- Avoiding emotions by using distractions such as work, mind- and mood-altering substances, or isolation.

- Constant anger or bitterness prevents you from experiencing joy.

- Prolonged numbness, where you feel disconnected from life.

- A deep sense of guilt, as though moving forward means betraying what was lost.

- Inability to form new relationships or engage in meaningful activities.

- Being "strong" for others by appearing unemotional and not allow yourself to "feel" the pain.

- Significant and prolonged disruptions in sleeping or eating habits—either excessive or insufficient.

- Continually refusing or avoiding help from friends, family, or support groups, often from feelings of pride, embarrassment, shame or guilt.

- Presenting a distorted or misleading picture of your life's actual condition—physically, financially, psychologically, and emotionally.

- Struggling to envision a meaningful future without the person or thing(s) that were lost, feeling uncertain about one's sense of self/identity.

- Consistent feelings of despair about the future, believing that happiness or relief will never return.

- Continuously replaying scenarios in one's mind, often wishing to reverse events or repeatedly imagining "what if" situations.

- Developing an increased fear of future losses, risk-taking, or change, resulting in hesitancy to make decisions or move forward.

- Persistently avoiding hobbies, interests, or social interactions that previously provided joy or comfort.

- Constantly revisiting conversations, events, or memories surrounding the loss without being able to accept closure or new perspectives.

- Trapped in the past—your conversations consistently circle around memories of people, places, moments, and things you've lost or deeply miss.

- Experiencing intense sadness or crying spells that don't lessen over time or become overwhelmed by seemingly minor triggers.

- Ongoing physical ailments such as headaches, fatigue, digestive issues, or muscle tension that have no clear medical cause, signaling unresolved emotional distress. Emotions not released will find a place to lodge in your physical body.

- Overly romanticizing or glorifying what or whom was lost, making it difficult to see any good in present circumstances or new opportunities without their presence.

- Continually refusing to acknowledge the reality or significance of the loss, even after considerable time has passed.

When grief lingers in a way that inhibits personal growth, it can lead to unhealthy coping mechanisms that make healing difficult.
Acknowledging where you are in the grieving process is the first step toward reclaiming your life. While grief never fully disappears, healing is

possible. It does not mean forgetting—it means learning to carry the memory of what or who you lost in a way that allows you to live again.

Grief: A Process, Not a Destination

Grief is a process, not a place we are meant to dwell indefinitely. It is an emotional response that demands to be felt, but it is not meant to define the rest of our lives. The way we process and navigate grief determines whether we emerge with a healed scar or an open wound that never closes.

A scar is evidence of healing. It is a mark that reminds us of what we have been through, but it no longer bleeds. The pain may have once been unbearable, but over time, it has transformed into something that no longer controls us. An open wound, however, is different; a wound unattended to leads to greater issues such as necrosis, reduced mobility, and a compromised immune system; so it is with unresolved grief as it can keep us stuck in patterns of avoidance, bitterness, depression, or self-destructive behaviors.

The Choice in Grief

While grief itself is not a choice, how we handle it is. Some people try to ignore it, stuffing their emotions down in an attempt to move on too quickly. Others dwell in it, refusing to release the pain, as if letting go means forgetting the one they lost. Some seek comfort in unhealthy coping mechanisms—turning to addictions - such as drugs, alcohol and food, or isolation from friends and family, or anger to numb the ache.

But there is another way. A way that acknowledges the pain but does not allow it to consume us. A way that honors what was lost while still embracing what remains. This is the path of healing, and it is one that requires intentionality, support, and surrender to God.

As we walk through the stages of grief together, I encourage you to reflect on where you are in your own journey. Have you allowed grief to heal as a scar, or are you still tending to an open wound? Do you recognize the ways in which you have tried to cope, and are they leading you toward healing or deeper pain?

Grief is inevitable, but being permanently broken by it is not. Healing is possible—but it begins with understanding the process and making the choice to move forward in a way that leads to restoration, rather than stagnation.

Grief is not only the loss of people but also the loss of things that held significance in our lives—such as jobs, homes, heirlooms, relationships, property, and pets. It is the mourning of anything that had value and a meaningful place in our lives but was stolen, taken or lost.

Grief progresses through seven stages, and if not properly processed, it can become a cycle that repeats itself. It is natural and necessary to mourn losses but lingering in an unhealthy level of grief can hinder you from moving forward in life.

I do not claim to be an expert on grief because of my higher education in counseling. I am educated on grief because I have personally experienced profound loss and learned how to overcome it—without carrying its unnecessary weight.

My Personal Experience

I have become deeply acquainted with grief—far more intimately than I ever wished to be. My journey with loss began painfully early. At age 7, I saw my grandmother draw her last breath as she had a heart attack on my bed. At age 15 years old, I lost my father to a cocaine overdose; he was only 37. A countless number of times from age 16-19 I witnessed the lifeless bodies of my peers taken far too soon to gun violence, at age 20 I mourned the passing of my cousin and best friend to an asthma attack and at age 21,1 experienced the unfulfilled promise of life when my pregnancy ended in miscarriage. I experienced prolonged grief watching my mother's life dwindle as she became a prisoner of her own body shortly before she was taken by ALS at age 56. I watched her brother - who was like a father to me - wither away to nothing as cancer riddled his body, and my grandmother to bone cancer. My heart shattered again when I grieved the profound loss of my child's father, mourning deeply for the devastating impact his absence had on our son, and I have stood too often at gravesides, bidding heartbreaking goodbyes to teenaged friends, aunts, and uncles—taken during vibrant years full of promise. I have lost boyfriends in my youth whose lives were taken, and a best friend, who was a sister, at the age of 50 to lupus.

I have whispered painful goodbyes to my fur-baby, whose passing coincided cruelly with my own battle with breast cancer, which claimed both of my breasts. My heart has ached over siblings whose lives ended prematurely through abortion, and divorce brought its own anguish and heaviness of heart.

I've felt the piercing sting of injustice as cherished family heirlooms and inheritances were stolen from me, properties that should have been passed on to me, and well-deserved career advancements repeatedly pulled from my grasp. Yet perhaps the deepest cut of all was grieving the irreplaceable years of motherhood lost due to my son's incarceration at age 15.

Loss creates a void and an emptiness that cannot be filled by anything in this world. And you cannot overcome it alone. If you do not know Jesus as Lord and Savior and have not received the gift of God—His Holy Spirit, who is our Comforter—it is impossible to truly overcome grief in a healthy way apart from Him. Those who seem to have moved past their grief without Llim have often only substituted it with something else, yet they still carry the pain of their loss.

Unhealthy Ways People Cope with Grief

It's understandable—human even—to seek relief from pain wherever it can be found, yet many paths we choose unknowingly deepen our wounds. Many attempt to cope with grief in ways that do more harm than good, including:

- **Alcohol:** Temporarily numbs feelings but ultimately increases emotional distress, health risks, co-dependency and addiction.

- **Drugs (prescribed or illegal):** Provide fleeting escape but lead to dependency and further harm.

- **Overworking (workaholism):** Distracts from grief yet isolates one from essential emotional support.

- **Becoming overly attached to others:** Attempts to fill emotional gaps, placing unhealthy expectations on relationships.

- **Isolation:** Seems protective but intensifies loneliness and despair and creates opportunities to plunge into deep depression.

- **Compulsive gravesite visits:** Reflects unresolved grief, preventing emotional closure.

- **Building shrines or monuments:** Though meant to honor, it often keeps individuals emotionally bound to the past and can become an altar to the deceased.

- **Necromancy (attempting communication with the deceased):** Spiritually harmful and leads to deception, entrapment and further away from genuine healing.

- **Depression:** Consumes joy and potential, making daily life difficult and sometimes undesirable.

- **Severely broken heart:** If left unaddressed, it evolves into prolonged emotional pain and dysfunction.

- **Loss or excessive increase in appetite:** Harms physical health and exacerbates emotional struggles.

- **Insomnia:** Denies essential rest, worsening emotional and mental health.

- **Avoiding emotions or "being strong":** Denies healing, leaving grief unresolved beneath the surface.

- **Emotional detachment:** Damages healthy relationships, leaving one isolated even among loved ones.

Grief is real, and loss is painful. But healing is possible through Jesus Christ, who gives peace beyond human understanding. With Him, you can move forward—not by forgetting, but by learning to live in freedom, carrying the love and lessons of those you have lost rather than the unbearable weight of grief.

This book will take you through the seven stages of grief, helping you identify where you are and how to navigate through grief in a way that fosters healing and transformation by using biblical examples to provide practical insights for your healing journey. Whether you are in the depths of sorrow or beginning to see glimpses of hope, know that God is with you, guiding you forward, and your story does not end with loss—there is still more ahead.

CHAPTER THREE

Shock & Denial — The First Blow Of Grief

The first stage of grief often begins with shock and denial, a natural protective mechanism allowing our minds and hearts time to process and cope with the overwhelming reality of loss. During this stage, we might feel numb, disconnected, or in disbelief; unable to fully accept the painful truth.

Shock is the immediate emotional reaction following a significant loss. It is characterized by an initial numbness that can leave individuals emotionally paralyzed and struggling to fully grasp or accept the reality of their situation. This stage often results in feelings of confusion, disorientation, and detachment from one's surroundings and emotions. We see this occur with David.

David's - Initial Shock of Absolom's Death

David experienced intense shock and denial upon hearing the devastating news that his rebellious son, Absalom, had been killed in battle. Despite Absalom's betrayal, David still deeply loved him. When he received the report of Absalom's death, David was visibly shaken, overwhelmed by grief, and unable to immediately accept the tragic outcome.

''The king was shaken. He went up to the room over the gateway and wept. As he went, he said: 'O my son Absalom! My son, my son Absalom! If only I had died instead of you—O Absalom, my son, my son!'" - 2 Samuel 18:33 (NIV)

David's reaction reveals profound emotional turmoil, clearly demonstrating signs of shock, disbelief, and intense grief as he struggled to accept the painful reality of losing his son, despite the complicated circumstances.

Jacob — Denial of Joseph's Death

Jacob experienced intense denial and shock upon hearing the news of his beloved son Joseph's supposed death. His sons presented Joseph's bloodied robe as evidence, and Jacob immediately spiraled into grief, refusing comfort from his family and remaining in a prolonged state of mourning and denial.

"Then Jacob tore his clothes, put on sackcloth and mourned for his son many days. All his sons and daughters came to comfort him, but he refused to be comforted. 'No,' he said, 'I will continue to mourn until I join my son in the grave.' So his father wept for him." - Genesis 37:34-35 (NIV)

Jacob's inability to accept Joseph's loss, evident through his persistent mourning and rejection of consolation, highlights the profound impact and depth of denial during grief.

The Effects of Shock and Denial

Shock and denial are the body's defense mechanisms against overwhelming pain. These mechanisms slow down emotional processing, allowing you to gradually face the full impact of grief. Some may feel numb, as if watching their life from afar, while others experience an overwhelming rush of conflicting emotions.

The effects of shock and denial vary from person to person, but some common experiences include:

- **Emotional numbness:** Feeling like you should be crying, but no tears will come or feeling detached or emotionally flat.

- **Disbelief and refusal to accept reality:** Insisting ''this can't be happening.''

- **Avoidance:** Actively avoiding conversations or reminders of the loss and continuing life as though the loss did not occur.

- **Minimizing the loss:** Downplaying the impact or seriousness of the event.

- **Confusion or disorientation:** Struggling to concentrate or make decisions.

- **Withdrawal from support networks:** Pulling away from friends and family.

- **Dizziness or lightheadedness:** A sense of being out of touch with reality.

- **Difficulty speaking or forming thoughts:** The brain feels foggy, making it hard to communicate.

- **Physical symptoms:** Heart palpitations, shallow breathing, shaking, headaches, fainting or stomach issues.

- **Repetitive behaviors:** Checking your phone to see if the person will call or text or you are calling or texting them, expecting them to walk through the door, or reliving the moment of loss over and over again.

Shock and denial can last for hours, days, or even weeks, depending on the individual and the situation as loss can be traumatizing. While it may seem like a numbing effect, it is a crucial part of the grieving process, giving the mind time to adjust before facing deeper emotions.

My Personal Experience

I know what shock and denial feels like. It has visited me more times than I would ever wish on anyone.

I was 15 years old when I lost my father. He was here one day and gone the next due to a drug overdose at the age of 37. The news came past 3 a.m., delivered through my mother after she received a phone call from my uncle. I remember hearing the words, but they didn't fully register. That morning, I got up, got dressed, and went to school like it was just another day. My mother even asked me if I wanted to stay home, but I told her no and walked out of the house as if nothing had changed. It wasn't until after my first-period class, while sitting in homeroom, that reality hit. I sat at my desk, unable to lift my head as I silently cried while my tears soaked the floor beneath me. The weight of my father's absence crushed me, and in that moment, shock released its grip, and pain took its place.

Years later, I would experience the same paralyzing effect when my son's father was taken from us. He was alive and well that day—my son had just spoken to him. I remember talking to my son on the phone, laughing and joking, ending the call on a joyful note. Then, minutes later, my son called back, his voice filled with tears and sorrow as he shared the news of how his father had been gunned down—killed by his supposed best friend. I could barely process it. One moment, life was normal, and the next, it had been shattered. I kept replaying the last conversation, the last words spoken, trying to grasp how something so permanent could happen in the blink of an eye.

Then, there was my best friend—more like a sister to me. We had been inseparable since the age of 15, thick as the skin of an alligator. She battled lupus for years and when struck with COVID, she overcame it, but the blood clots that followed took her life. Even though I stood at her funeral and served as the master of ceremony, I still couldn't believe she was gone. I was in shock for almost a year; waiting for a call that would never come, expecting to see her name pop up on my phone, struggling to accept that our late-night talks, coded-inside jokes and shared laughter were now just memories.

And then, there was my mother. Her passing was different because it was expected but still just as shocking. She was diagnosed with ALS, and I watched as she became imprisoned in her body. Even though I knew it was coming, even though I had prepared for it, the finality of it still sent me into shock.

There are far too many more experiences like these; each one leaving a scar in my heart, but through the grace and comfort of God I was able to overcome.

Unhealthy Responses to Shock & Denial

Because shock is such an overwhelming experience, many people instinctively seek ways to numb the pain further. This can lead to unhealthy coping mechanisms such as:

- **Avoidance:** Pretending the loss never happened, refusing to talk about it, or throwing oneself into work or distractions.

- **Substance use:** Using alcohol, drugs, or even excessive food consumption to suppress emotions.

- **Over-functioning:** Taking on unnecessary responsibilities to stay busy and avoid dealing with feelings.

- **Isolation:** Withdrawing from friends, family, or community support.

- **Anger and blame:** Lashing out at others, blaming medical professionals, or even blaming God.

- **Hyper-Control:** Becoming obsessively controlling about minor details or routines in an attempt to regain a sense of security and normalcy.

- **Risky or Impulsive Behaviors:** Engaging in reckless activities such as impulsive spending, gambling, reckless driving, or unsafe sexual behavior as a distraction from emotional pain.

- **Excessive digital escape:** Excessive scrolling, gaming, binge-watching movies or TV, or other digital distractions.

- **Emotional Numbness or Dissociation:** Detaching emotionally and mentally from reality, resulting in feeling disconnected from oneself or one's surroundings.

- **Self-Harm or Neglect:** Intentionally harming oneself physically or neglecting basic self-care as an unhealthy coping mechanism to process intense emotional pain or guilt.

- **Compulsive Behaviors:** Developing obsessive or compulsive patterns like excessive cleaning, hoarding, or repetitive checking, driven by underlying anxiety and shock.

- **Chronic Worry or Anxiety:** Constantly anticipating further tragedy, obsessing over ''worst-case scenarios,'' and living in continual fear, creating significant emotional exhaustion.

- **Overdependence on Others:** Becoming overly reliant or clingy toward certain individuals, believing one cannot survive or function without constant external validation or support.

- **Prolonged Victimhood or Helplessness:** Getting stuck in a mindset of helplessness or victimhood, feeling unable or unwilling to take any proactive steps toward healing or recovery.

- **Spiritual Crisis or Despair:** Experiencing profound despair or bitterness toward one's faith-based beliefs or community, resulting in abandonment or rejection of former sources of comfort or strength.

- **Projection onto Others:** Projecting one's pain or unresolved emotions onto others, misplacing anger or frustration, and inadvertently damaging relationships.

While these responses may provide temporary relief and false peace, they only delay the grieving process. Pain is not healed by time; emotional and mental healing flows from the embrace of a loving and compassionate Heavenly Father who heals the brokenhearted and binds up their wounds [curing their pains and their sorrows]. Psalm 147:3.

Signs of Shock and Grief in Children

Many times, we are so focused on our own grief that we miss identifying children who struggle with loss.

Children may experience similar or different signs of shock and grief that you will need to identify to assist them with the journey into healing with a pastor or counselor.

Children experiencing shock and grief often exhibit unique signs, including rebellious behavior. Here are several key signs to look out for:

Emotional and Behavioral Signs

1. **Rebellion and Defiance:** Showing anger, resisting authority, breaking rules, or engaging in risky behaviors as a way to regain control.

2. **Regression:** Returning to earlier developmental behaviors such as bedwetting, thumb-sucking, or clinginess.

3. **Withdrawal or Isolation:** avoiding friends, family, or previously enjoyed activities, becoming unusually quiet or secretive.

4. **Anger and Irritability:** Having frequent emotional outbursts or tantrums, becoming easily irritated, frustrated, or hostile.

5. **Anxiety or Excessive Worry:** Persistent fearfulness, worrying about the safety of loved ones, or becoming overly cautious.

6. **Sudden Academic or Performance Decline:** Loss of interest in schoolwork, poor concentration, or a drop in academic performance.

Physical Signs:

7. **Sleep Disturbances:** Nightmares, trouble falling asleep, or excessive sleeping.

8. **Changes in Eating Habits:** Significant increase or decrease in appetite, or frequent stomachaches or headaches without clear medical cause.

Social Signs:

9. **Aggression Towards Peers or Siblings:** Increased fighting, stealing, bullying behaviors, or blaming others.

10. **Attention-Seeking Behaviors:** Acting out, being overly demanding, or craving constant attention from adults.

Psychological Signs:

11. **Feelings of Guilt or Self-Blame:** Expressing thoughts that the loss is their fault or showing low self-esteem.

12. **Difficulty Expressing Feelings:** Struggling to talk about the loss, suppressing emotions, or becoming unusually silent when asked about their feelings.

Spiritual Signs:

13. **Questioning Faith or Spiritual Beliefs:** Displaying anger toward God or confusion as to why He did not stop it from happening.

Why These Signs Occur:

Children often don't have the language or emotional maturity to clearly express grief. Rebellion and other behaviors can emerge as they struggle internally to understand and process their emotions. They may use these behaviors to communicate their pain, fear, confusion, and need for reassurance.

Helpful Approaches:

- **Patience and Understanding:** Validate their feelings, even if expressed negatively.

- **Open Communication:** Create safe, non-judgmental spaces for honest conversations.

- **Reassurance and Routine:** Maintain structure and predictable routines to give children stability and safety.

- **Professional Support:** Counseling or therapy can provide specialized guidance to children struggling to cope effectively.

Recognizing and responding compassionately to these signs can help guide children toward healing and emotional resilience.

Breaking Through Shock in a Healthy Way

While shock is a necessary initial response to grief, staying in this stage for too long can prevent healing. To move beyond shock and denial effectively, it is essential to adopt healthy coping strategies:

- **Acknowledge Your Feelings:** Allow yourself to experience emotions without judgment.

- **Connect with Support Networks:** Seek comfort and support from family, friends, or support groups.

- **Express Your Emotions:** Talk openly about your grief, journal, or engage in creative activities.

- **Maintain Healthy Routines:** Regular meals, exercise, rest, and self-care help restore a sense of normalcy.

- **Seek Godly Support:** Engage in prayer, meditating on God's Word, or Pastoral/Christian counsel to find peace and guidance.

True healing occurs by consciously facing grief, processing emotions authentically, and gradually moving forward toward emotional restoration and renewal.

Shock and denials is not meant to be permanent. It is a doorway into the grieving process, not a place to remain. If you find yourself stuck, unable to move forward, it may be time to seek guidance from a trusted counselor, pastor, or support group.

Prayer to Overcome Shock and Denial

Heavenly Father,

My heart feels overwhelmed, and my mind struggles to accept this loss that is causing me to feel lost. Yet, Lord, I am coming to you, because You are my refuge and strength, a very present help in trouble. When I am tossed by confusion and numbness, anchor me in Your unchanging truth.

You are the God who heals the brokenhearted and brings light into every dark place. Right now, I do not understand, so help me to trust You with all my heart and not lean on my own understanding. Heal my heart and the wounds this loss left that I do not have the words to express, and bring peace to the chaos raging inside me.

Father, I renounce the grip of denial and ask for Your Spirit of truth to guide me gently into acceptance of what has happened at the pace You know I can handle. Wrap me in Your arms and carry me through this valley. Strengthen me to face reality, not by my own might, but by Your Spirit working within me.

Holy Spirit, when I feel disoriented and lost, remind me that I am never abandoned. I know that You are a Comforter and Counselor and right now, at this very moment, I need you as both. Speak to my heart, give me courage for each next step, teach me to give every care and concern to You, because You care for me with a love that will never let me go.

Jesus, You are acquainted with grief and sorrow. You understand shock and loss, and You stood victorious over it all. Help me fix my eyes on You—the Author and Finisher of my faith—so that despair does not consume me, but that Your hope will arise and sustain me.

Father, breathe fresh strength into my weary spirit. Help me to be still and know that You are God. I declare by faith that You are working all things together for the good, even when I cannot yet see it. I submit my pain, my fear, my questions—and even my denial—into Your faithful hands.

Thank You for being patient with me Lord. Thank You for making a way through what feels impossible. I declare today that you are my

Healer, my Fortress, and my Deliverer. I will wait upon You, and I believe I will see Your goodness in my life again. In Jesus' mighty name, Amen.

Moving Forward

The first stage of grief is often the most disorienting because it challenges everything we know about life and security. But even in the midst of shock & denial, there is hope. The fact that grief exists means that love existed first. And while the pain of loss is real, it does not have to define you forever.

In the next chapter, we will explore **Pain & Guilt** — be mindful that shock and denial may occur at the same time as pain and guilt, as there is no specific order in which you will experience these emotions resulting from loss.

.

CHAPTER FOUR

Pain And Guilt — The Heavy Burden Of Grief

If shock is the initial numbing of grief, then pain and guilt are the first true signs that grief has begun to settle into the soul. This stage of grief is often the most emotionally overwhelming because it forces us to confront the reality of what has been lost. While shock protects us momentarily from the full brunt of sorrow, once that shield fades, we are left to deal with the raw emotions that follow.

The Depth of Pain in Grief

Pain in grief is not just an emotion—it is a full-body experience. It can feel like an invisible weight pressing down on the chest, making it hard to breathe. It can manifest as an ache deep within, one that no medication or remedy can ease. Some describe it as drowning in an ocean of sorrow, struggling to keep their head above water, or feeling lost and disoriented as if the path of life was snatched from under their feet, while others feel constant emptiness, a void that no distraction can fill.

Pain is inevitable in grief, and while it may seem unbearable, it serves a purpose. Pain reminds us that what we lost mattered, that the love or connection we had was real. But pain, if not processed in a healthy way, can also lead to despair. It can cause us to withdraw from life, avoid relationships, or live in a state of sadness that feels impossible to escape.

Pain must be acknowledged, but it must not be allowed to consume us. Healing begins when we learn how to sit with our pain, recognize its presence, and allow it to guide us forward rather than keep us trapped in sorrow.

David — Overwhelmed with grief

King David experienced profound pain and guilt after losing his child born from his relationship with Bathsheba. His pain was compounded by guilt over his own sins—adultery and the orchestrated death of Bathsheba's husband, Uriah. David openly expressed his sorrow and guilt, turning to God in heartfelt repentance.

"My guilt has overwhelmed me like a burden too heavy to bear." - Psalm 38:4 (NIV)

Peter — Pain of Guilt

Peter experienced intense pain and overwhelming guilt after denying Jesus three times, exactly as Jesus had predicted. His grief was immediate and profound, marked by deep regret and self-condemnation, driving him to weep bitterly.

"Then Peter remembered the word Jesus had spoken: 'Before the rooster crows, you will disown me three times.' And he went outside and wept bitterly." - Matthew 26:75 (NIV)

Effects of Pain and Guilt

Pain and guilt profoundly impact our emotional, mental, and spiritual well-being. They can manifest as:

- Persistent sadness and crying spells
- Overwhelming feelings of self-blame and regret
- Loss of appetite and sleep disturbances
- Feelings of worthlessness or hopelessness
- Withdrawal from relationships and social activities

• Difficulty performing daily tasks

My Personal Experience

I cannot begin to describe the overwhelming pain I felt in 1994 when a male friend's life was suddenly taken. It pierced deeply into my heart, leaving a wound so intense that I found myself playing the same song on repeat that reinforced and even nurtured my sorrow for months because the pain was so intense that I did not wish to face the reality of his absence in my life.

On the day my grandmother passed away from a heart attack, she had asked me to get her medication, but I was too absorbed in playing with my brother and chose not to stop. For years afterward, throughout my childhood and into my young adulthood, I was haunted by thoughts of guilt that her death was entirely my fault. "If only I had stopped and brought her the medication," I repeated to myself countless times, believing deeply that my simple choice could have saved her life. The weight of that guilt lingered until the Lover of my soul; Jesus, set me free.

Unhealthy Responses to Pain and Guilt

When overwhelmed, people may respond in unhealthy ways:

- Persistent self-blame or shame
- Isolation from supportive relationships
- Substance abuse to numb pain
- Avoiding necessary grief processing
- Engaging in self-destructive behaviors
- Excessive busyness or workaholism to avoid facing emotions
- Excessive sleep or prolonged inactivity as an escape
- Negative self-talk or constant self-criticism
- Seeking validation through unhealthy relationships or behaviors
- Spiritual withdrawal or bitterness towards faith or spiritual communities
- Angry with God.

Signs of Pain and Guilt in Children

Children experiencing pain and guilt may show:

- Regression to earlier developmental behaviors
- Increased aggression or irritability
- Difficulty sleeping or frequent nightmares
- Clinginess or excessive attachment to caregivers
- Withdrawal from friends and usual activities
- Sudden academic or performance decline
- Persistent anxiety or fearfulness
- Expressions of self-blame or worthlessness
- Physical complaints (headaches, stomachaches) without medical causes
- Frequent emotional outbursts or crying spells

Healing or Despair?

Pain and guilt have the power to take us in one of two directions: they can push us toward healing, or they can pull us into despair. How we handle these emotions determines which path we take.

- **Despair looks like:**

  o Constantly replaying moments we regret, refusing to forgive ourselves.

  o Withdrawing from life, feeling unworthy of happiness,

  o Self-Pity

  o Becoming a martyr by carrying guilt as a personal punishment, as if suffering will somehow make things right.

  o Avoiding grief altogether, using work, substances, or distractions to numb the pain.

- **Healing looks like:**

  o Acknowledging our pain instead of running from it.

o Understanding that guilt often lies to us, making us believe we had control over things we never had control over.

o Seeking support—whether through counseling, pastoral care or trusted friends—to help process emotions.

o Learning on the Holy Spirit as a Comforter.

o Learning to offer ourselves the same grace we would extend to others.

o Praising God through the pain - this is a difficult one to receive and accept, but it is acknowledging that though the state of your heart is not good, He is.

One of the hardest but most necessary steps in grief is accepting that we are not in control of life and death. We cannot change the past, but we can choose how we carry it forward. Pain and guilt will visit us all in grief, but they do not have to become permanent residents in our hearts.

Letting Go of Guilt and Embracing Healing

Healing begins when we forgive ourselves. It begins when we stop punishing ourselves for things we cannot change and start allowing grace to fill the spaces where guilt once lived. It does not mean forgetting. It does not mean that the loss stops hurting. But it does mean that we stop carrying burdens that were never meant to be ours.

If you are struggling with guilt, I encourage you to take a moment to ask yourself: **Am I holding myself accountable for something that was never truly my responsibility?** And if the answer is yes, I urge you to begin the process of letting it go. Not because the loss doesn't matter, but because your healing does.

Prayer for Healing from Pain and Guilt in Grief

Gracious Father,

I come before You with a heavy heart, pierced with pain and guilt. The pain of my loss runs deep, and at times, I find myself replaying moments, wondering what I could have done differently. Lord, I lay these thoughts before You—the regrets, the questions, the pain, void and guilt.

You are the God who sees, the One who understands every unspoken ache. You know the depth of my sorrow and the weight of the guilt I carry. But today, I choose to run into Your arms, where mercy triumphs over judgment and grace covers every shortcoming. I thank You that in Christ, there is no condemnation.

Help me, Lord, to release what I cannot change and receive Your peace that surpasses all understanding. Heal the wounds I've carried too long. Let Your truth silence the voice of guilt and remind me that Your love does not keep score of wrongs.

Restore my soul, O God. Bind up what's been broken by sorrow and shame. Let the comfort of Your presence be greater than the pain of my loss. Where guilt has clouded my vision, clear my eyes with Your compassion. Where pain has hardened my heart, soften me again with Your love.

Holy Spirit, help me to forgive myself and walk in the freedom that Jesus died to give me. Give me the strength to cherish the memories without being chained to regret. Let me remember the good, honor the past, and move forward with hope.

I surrender every unanswered question to You, Father and I trust You to carry me through this valley. Thank You for never leaving me alone in my grief. You are my Refuge, my Healer, and my Ever-present help. In the name of Jesus, Amen.

Moving Forward

Moving forward involves intentionally applying healthy coping strategies—such as acknowledging your emotions, seeking support, practicing forgiveness of self, others who may have caused the loss of things that he held dear to you or even the person that passed, and engaging in self-care and mindfulness. As you gradually come to terms with the realities of pain and guilt, you will be better prepared for the days to come. Remember, grief does not always unfold sequentially; these stages may occur simultaneously or in varying orders, and some stages may even be skipped entirely. However your journey unfolds, the conscious choice to move forward equips you to handle grief authentically and effectively, paving the way for deeper healing and restoration.

Pain and guilt will always be a part of grief, but they do not have to define your journey. In the next chapter, we will explore the next stage of grief—**anger and bargaining**—and how the search for answers and justice can often complicate the healing process.

CHAPTER FIVE

Anger And Bargaining: The Fight For Answers

Following shock, denial, pain, and guilt, grief may transition into bargaining and anger. Bargaining typically involves attempting to negotiate a way out of loss or to lessen its emotional toll, often through promises or appeals to God. Anger arises from feelings of injustice, powerlessness, or frustration over the inability to control or reverse the loss. This stage of grief is turbulent, filled with frustration, resentment, and an overwhelming sense of unfairness. If left unchecked, anger can harden the heart, and bargaining can leave a person stuck in an endless loop of *what-ifs* and *if onlys.*

David — Battle with Bargaining

After David committed adultery with Bathsheba and orchestrated the death of her husband Uriah, the prophet Nathan confronted him. David confessed his sin, and while God forgave him, the consequence of his actions was that the child born from that union would die.

When the child became ill, David entered a period of intense bargaining. He fasted, wept, and lay all night on the ground, refusing food or comfort. He pleaded with God to spare the child, hoping his repentance and humility might change the outcome. This was a clear stage of bargaining, a desperate effort to reverse the consequence of his loss.

"David therefore appealed to God for the child [to be healed]; and David fasted *went in and lay all night on the ground* — **2 Samuel 12:16 AMP**

'Then his servants said to him, "What is this thing that you have done? While the *child was alive you fasted and wept, but when the child died, you got up and ate* *food. " David said, 'While the child was still alive, I fasted and wept; for i thought,* *Who knows, the Lord may be gracious to me and the child may live".* — **2** **Samuel 12:21 AMP**

Cain — Anger and Loss

Cain experienced a deep emotional loss—not the death of a loved one, but the loss of divine approval and relational acceptance. When both Cain and Abel brought offerings to the Lord, God accepted Abel's offering but rejected Cain's. This rejection triggered anger, jealousy, and offense in Cain's heart.

Instead of turning to God for correction or realignment, Cain internalized the loss as personal failure and injustice, fueling a rage that led him to murder his brother Abel. His anger became destructive because it was unresolved and rooted in wounded pride, insecurity, and the perceived loss of favor.

The Lord, in His mercy, warned Cain: "ILTry *are you angry?"* and instructed him to rule over the sin that was waiting to consume him. But Cain allowed his grief over lost validation to turn into vengeance.

Cain's story reveals that loss doesn't always come from physical death—it can come from rejection, comparison, or unmet expectations. And when loss is left unchecked, it can breed anger that spirals into devastation.

... but on Cain and his offering he did not look with favor. So Cain was very angry *and his face was downcast. Then the Lord said to Cain, 'Why are you angry? Why* *is your face downcast? If you do what is right, will you not be accepted? But if you* *not do what is right, sin is crouching at your door; it desires to have you, but you* *must rule over it. " Genesis 4:5-7 (NIV)*

Effects of Bargaining and Anger

Bargaining and anger significantly influence emotional and spiritual well-being. Common effects include:

- Feelings of frustration and resentment
- Heightened irritability and anger outbursts
- Attempts at negotiating unrealistic deals or promises
- Emotional exhaustion and persistent tension
- Strained relationships due to conflict or withdrawal
- Physical symptoms like headaches, muscle tension, or fatigue

My Personal Experience

I know what it means to be consumed by anger as well as walk the path of bargaining desperately wishing to trade one reality for another. When my father died, I wasn't just heartbroken—I was furious. And my anger had a target: my mother.

At 15 years old, I made the decision to leave home, fueled by the deep resentment I held toward her. I blamed her for keeping me from my father, for denying him access to me. I told myself that if she hadn't placed a wedge between us, I would have had more time with him; that I would have been his reason to live and that I wouldn't have grown up without his presence in my life.

I saw my mother as the villain, someone who only wanted me to move back in her home from my father's home, not because she truly wanted to rebuild a relationship with me, but so she could receive child support payments. I held onto that bitterness for years, allowing it to harden me, and shape the way I viewed her and our relationship. My grief had turned into rage, and that rage took root in my words and thoughts.

I spoke ill-wishes over of my mother, and in the depths of my pain, I even bargained and wished it had been her instead of my father. I convinced myself that if I could trade one life for another, the world would be made right again. Looking back now, I see the cruelty and harshness of my thoughts, but at the time, I was just a broken little girl who had lost her father and didn't know how to process the storm of emotions inside me.

That wasn't the only time anger consumed me. When my son's father was violently taken from us, my grief turned into a rage that embraced retaliation. I wanted vengeance towards the man who stole my son's father from him, for the pain that was inflicted upon my child. The anger I felt was no longer just my own—it was as if I carried the weight of loss for both my son and myself. Seeing my teenager fall into a state of sorrow that led to anger only intensified my own fury. I felt helpless watching him navigate grief so deep. I wanted the supposed best friend to pay. I wanted him to feel the same pain we were experiencing, but anger never brings healing—it only fuels destruction. I had to learn to release it, not for them, but for me, for my son, and for our ability to heal beyond the loss.

It took years for me to understand the damage that anger and bargaining had done to my soul. It wasn't just my mother who suffered because of my resentment—I suffered too. The weight of that anger drained me, kept me from fully experiencing joy, and clouded my ability to move forward. Healing only began when I acknowledged the pain beneath the anger and allowed myself to grieve without needing someone to blame.

Unhealthy Responses to Bargaining and Anger

Unhealthy responses may include:

- Persistent blaming of self or others
- Engaging in destructive or aggressive behaviors
- Excessive isolation or withdrawal from relationships
- Resorting to substance abuse as a coping mechanism
- Holding onto grudges or unresolved bitterness
- Persistent denial of the reality of the loss
- Releasing ill-wishes or witchcraft prayers over others

Signs of Bargaining and Anger in Children

Children experiencing bargaining and anger may exhibit:

- Frequent temper tantrums or aggressive behaviors
- Difficulty controlling emotions or impulses
- Expressing unrealistic wishes or promises to reverse the loss
- Increased irritability or frustration
- Withdrawal or conflict with peers and adults
- Blaming themselves or others repeatedly
- Sudden changes in behavior or academic performance
- Suicidal thoughts - feeling life is not worth living

The Role of Anger in Grief

Anger is often misunderstood in grief. It is not just an emotional outburst—it is a defense mechanism, a way to push back against the pain that feels too immense to face. The anger may be directed toward oneself, toward others, toward God, or even toward the one who passed away. It can stem from feelings of abandonment, injustice, or regret. Some lash out in obvious ways, through aggression or destructive behaviors, while others internalize it, allowing resentment to quietly corrode their peace.

While anger is a natural part of grieving, it becomes dangerous when it is never processed or released. It can destroy relationships, lead to unhealthy coping mechanisms, and keep the grieving person imprisoned in bitterness rather than moving toward healing.

The Desperation of Bargaining

Bargaining is the mind's attempt to negotiate with reality, to rewrite the past or alter the future in a desperate bid to escape the pain of loss. It is filled with *if only* statements:

- If only I had been there sooner, maybe they would still be alive.

- If only I had done things differently, maybe this wouldn't have happened.

- If only I had been a better daughter, son, friend, or spouse, maybe they wouldn't have left me.

- If only I knew what they were battling I could have helped.

Some people direct their bargaining toward God, making deals in an attempt to reverse what has already been done. Others compare losses, wishing that someone else had died instead of their loved one. The bargaining stage is often intertwined with guilt, as people try to assign responsibility for the loss, even when none truly exists.

The Dangers of Unresolved Anger and Bargaining

When anger and bargaining remain unchecked, they can take us down a path of destruction. Some dangers of remaining in this stage of grief include:

- **Broken Relationships -** Anger can push away the very people who want to help and support us.

- **Self-Destruction -** Holding onto anger can lead to self-sabotaging behaviors such as substance abuse, isolation, or reckless decisions.

- **A Distorted Perspective of God and Life -** Bargaining often leads to disappointment with God when He does not grant the desperate deals we make in grief.

- **Emotional Numbness -** Over time, holding onto anger can lead to emotional exhaustion, making it harder to feel anything at all.

- **Savior Complex -** Thinking that you had the power and the ability to prevent what occurred - "If only I had...".

Process Anger and Bargaining in a Healthy Way

Moving through the stage of anger and bargaining requires intentionality. It is not about suppressing these emotions but about releasing them in a way that does not cause further harm. Here are a few steps toward healing:

- **Express Emotions Constructively:** Share feelings openly with trusted individuals, pastors or counselors.

- **Seek Godly Counsel:** Pray and meditate on scripture for peace and perspective.

- **Stay Connected:** Maintain supportive relationships to avoid isolation.

- **Prioritize Healthy Activities:** Regular exercise, adequate sleep, and healthy nutrition.

- **Pursue Professional Support:** Seek counseling or therapy to gain coping skills and emotional clarity.

- **Acknowledge the Anger:** Recognize it for what it is: an expression of pain, not a solution to it.

- **Find a Safe Outlet:** Talk to a trusted friend or journal your emotions to process them constructively.

- **Forgive, Even When It Feels Impossible:** Forgive the person that left you, or the person that you hold responsible for the loss such as a doctor, accoster, etc. Forgiveness is not excusing wrongdoing but about freeing yourself from the chains of resentment and torment.

- **Pray and Release It to God:** If faith is a part of your life, surrendering anger and bargaining to God can bring peace where there was once only turmoil.

- **Shift the Perspective:** Instead of asking, **"Why did this happen?"**, start asking, **"How can I heal from this?"**

Prayer to Overcome Bargaining and Anger in Grief

Heavenly Father,

I am hurting, and cannot seem to shake what I am feeling, and to be honest, I don't know if I want to. I am angry. I am angry towards You for allowing this to happen, I am angry with the person who caused this loss and I am angry that I cannot go back in time and fix this, I am angry that I did not get to say all the things I wanted to say or receive closure **(if there is anything else you are angry about add it here)** because my heart aches for what was lost and what will never be the same. I don't understand why this happened the way it did. The unanswered questions stirs frustration within me, but I bring it all before You, my Righteous and Merciful God. I know You are not intimidated by my emotions, so I thank you for being patient and gentle, even when I am not.

Lord, help me process this anger in Your presence instead of allowing it to take root and grow into bitterness. Heal the wounds beneath the rage—the sorrow, the regret, and the helplessness. Your word says You are close to the brokenhearted, and You save those who are crushed in spirit. I ask You now to calm the storm inside me. Teach me to be slow to anger, and quick to turn to You for peace.

Father, I give You my anger. I surrender the need to make sense of everything and invite You Holy Spirit to take the lead. Transform my grief into grace, and my rage into rest. Let Your Word renew my mind and Your love soften my heart. I am choosing to trust You, even through the questions. Thank you for not allowing me to be consumed by anger and thank You for walking with me through the valley of grief, and for leading me toward peace. In Jesus Name.

Moving Forward

Letting go of anger does not mean forgetting. It does not mean pretending the pain is gone. It simply means choosing to no longer let grief make you a prisoner to rage and regret.

If you find yourself in this stage of grief, I urge you to ask yourself: **"Is my anger serving me, or is it keeping me stuck?"** Healing begins when we make the choice to move forward, even when we don't feel ready.

In the next chapter, we will explore the next stage of grief— **depression**—and how the weight of loss can lead us into isolation, sadness, and a struggle to find hope again.

CHAPTER SIX

Depression — The Valley Of Grief

When anger fades and bargaining fails to rewrite the past, grief often settles into a heavy and consuming sorrow known as depression. The world keeps moving forward, yet the grieving person feels stuck in time, unable to engage with life the way they once did.

This stage of grief is different from everyday sadness—it is an overwhelming emotional weight that can make even the simplest tasks feel impossible. Depression in grief is often accompanied by a deep sense of loneliness, hopelessness, and emotional numbness. It is often accompanied by deep emotional exhaustion and can manifest in varying degrees—from mild sadness and melancholy to severe clinical depression characterized by prolonged despair, withdrawal, and thoughts of self-harm or suicide.

While depression in grief is natural, remaining in this stage for too long can be dangerous. Understanding this stage is crucial to finding a way out of the darkness and into healing.

The Levels of Depression in Grief

Depression in grief manifests in different levels, ranging from temporary sadness to debilitating despair. These levels can fluctuate, and individuals may move between them over time:

1. **Mild Depression:** Feelings of sadness, fatigue, and disinterest in activities once enjoyed. Life feels dull, but functioning is still possible.

2. **Moderate Depression:** Persistent feelings of emptiness, withdrawal from social interactions, difficulty focusing, and an overall loss of motivation.

3. **Severe Depression:** A deep emotional numbness, overwhelming hopelessness, thoughts of self-harm or suicide, substance abuse, and complete disengagement from life.

Each level requires attention and care. What may begin as mild depression can quickly spiral into something more severe if left unaddressed.

Elijah - Battle with Depression

After facing threats to his life from Queen Jezebel, Elijah fell into a deep state of depression. He isolated himself, felt profoundly hopeless, and wished for death.

"He came to a broom bush, sat down under it, and prayed that he might die. 'I *had enough, LORD,' he said. Dake my life; I am no better than my ancestors. "*
1 Kings 19:4 (NIV)

Naomi - Stricken with Sorrow

Naomi experienced severe depression after losing her husband and sons. She described her emotional state as bitter and empty, unable to see hope or joy in her future.

'Don't call me Naomi,' she told them. 'Call me Mara, because the Almighty has *made my life very bitter. I went away full, but the LORD has brought me back* *empty."*— Ruth 1:20-21 (NIV)

Job — Death Wish

Job gives voice to one of the clearest biblical expressions of despair and depression. After suffering immense and sudden loss—his children, his wealth, and his health—Job plunges into a state of emotional anguish so deep that he wishes he had never been born. This is not a fleeting thought, but the cry of a man overwhelmed by sorrow and internal suffering. Job curses the day he was born in Job chapter 3 verses 1-10 leading up to verse 11.

"Why did I not perish at birth, and die as I came from the womb? Job 3:11 (NIV)

Effects and the Role of Depression

Depression serves as a painful yet critical stage of grief, allowing individuals to fully acknowledge their loss. It impacts every area of life, including physical health, emotional stability, spiritual well-being, and relationships. Common effects include:

Cognitive Effects:

- Negative self-talk or excessive self-criticism
- Memory problems or forgetfulness
- Indecisiveness or slowed thinking
- Rumination (obsessive focus on distressing thoughts)

Physical Symptoms:

- Aches and pains with no clear physical cause (headaches, back pain, stomach issues)
- Weakened immune system (more susceptible to illness)
- Changes in motor function (slowed movement or speech, known as psychomotor retardation)
- Weight gain or loss unrelated to diet
- Reduced libido or sexual dysfunction

Behavioral Signs:

- Neglect of responsibilities (work, school, hygiene, parenting etc.)
- Increased substance use (alcohol, drugs, nicotine, prescription drugs)
- Self-harm (cutting, burning, etc.)
- Suicidal thoughts or behaviors
- Avoidance of enjoyable activities (anhedonia)

Emotional/Interpersonal Effects:

- Irritability or anger outbursts, even over small matters
- Feelings of worthlessness, guilt, or being a burden
- Difficulty feeling joy even during positive experiences
- Over-dependence on others or complete emotional detachment

My Personal Experience

At age 15, I found myself drowning in this stage of grief for eight years. What began as sadness over the losses I had endured evolved into a darkness I could not shake. Depression took hold of me, and instead of finding healthy ways to cope, I turned to the very things that would keep me trapped in my pain.

I sought escape in drugs—both illegal and prescription—mixing them with alcohol as I was seeking a means of escape - even if it were death. The weight of my grief was unbearable, and promiscuity, lewd living, lawlessness and substance abuse became my norm.

For years, I functioned through life carrying a secret war within me, and my coping mechanisms only deepened my sorrow. Depression led me down a road of reckless self-destruction. I became suicidal, placing myself in harm's way on a regular basis. I felt like I had no purpose, and no real reason to keep going. The pain was so deep that I began engaging in dangerous behaviors, not caring whether I lived or died.

In my desperate search for the love I lost with my father's death, I sought comfort in relationships with older men—some old enough to be my father. I was looking for something to fill the void, to replace the love and security I had been robbed of, but those relationships only deepened my brokenness. They could not give me the love I was craving because it was a wound no one but God could truly heal.

Looking back now, I see how my grief had arrested my development, keeping me trapped in the past, unable to fully engage with the present. The stage of depression had lasted far too long, and I was unable to pull myself out of it alone. My journey of finding hope truly began when I gave my life to Jesus at age 22. It was the first time I surrendered the burdens I had been carrying and receiving freedom from the weight of depression.

Signs of Depression in Children

Children experiencing depression may exhibit:

- Persistent sadness or frequent crying
- Withdrawal from friends, family, or social activities
- Sudden drop in academic performance
- Changes in appetite and sleep patterns
- Physical complaints without a medical cause
- Expressions of hopelessness or worthlessness
- Unkempt appearance; poor personal hygiene
- Increased irritability or agitation

Negative Coping Mechanisms in This Stage

Many people develop unhealthy coping mechanisms in an attempt to numb or escape the pain of depression. These can include:

- **Substance Abuse:** Turning to alcohol, illegal drugs, or prescription medication to dull the pain.

- **Isolation:** Withdrawing from friends, family, and support systems, choosing solitude over connection.

- **Gaming:** Many times excessive and over use of video games such as Xbox or PlayStation can be an addiction used as a means of escaping reality.

- **Overworking:** Burying oneself in work to avoid dealing with emotions.

- **Reckless Behavior:** Engaging in dangerous activities, impulsive spending, or unhealthy relationships to distract from the pain.

- **Self-Harm:** Inflicting physical pain to counteract emotional pain or as a cry for help.

- **Denial:** Pretending to be fine, masking grief with a smile while suffering internally.

While these coping mechanisms may provide temporary relief, they ultimately prolong the suffering and make healing even more difficult.

How People Camouflage Depression

One of the most deceptive aspects of this stage is how well people learn to camouflage it. Depression does not always look like someone lying in bed all day. People can be highly functional in their sadness, hiding their grief behind carefully crafted facades. Some common ways people mask their depression include:

- **Becoming the "Strong One":** Always helping others but never acknowledging their own pain.

- **Humor as a Defense Mechanism:** Using jokes and laughter to distract from inner turmoil.

- **Busyness as a Shield:** Filling every moment with obligations to avoid sitting with their emotions.

- **Social Media Perfection:** Posting happy, filtered moments while privately suffering.

- **Subtle Self-Sabotage:** Making poor choices that reinforce feelings of worthlessness.

- **Perfectionism:** Constantly striving for unrealistic standards to avoid confronting inner feelings of inadequacy.

- **Excessive Optimism:** Projecting positivity to hide deep emotional struggles.

- **Physical Appearance Obsession:** Focusing excessively on appearance as a distraction from emotional pain.

- **Overachieving:** Continuously pushing oneself to succeed as a means of validating self-worth.

- **Excessive Spending:** Can be a sign of depression — though it's often overlooked. It falls under **impulsive or escapist behavior,** which some individuals use to temporarily relieve emotional pain or to numb feelings of emptiness, sadness, or anxiety as it provides a **Dopamine boost:** a short-term "high" or sense of control.

  o **Avoidance:** It serves as a distraction from distressing thoughts or feelings.

  o **Self-soothing:** People may spend to compensate for low self-worth or to feel momentarily "better."

- **This can also include Unipolar depression:**
  o Unipolar depression is the clinical term for major depressive disorder (MDD) — a mood disorder characterized by a persistent, prolonged low mood and loss of interest or pleasure in most activities. It's called *unipolar* because, unlike bipolar disorder, it does not include episodes of mania or hypomania — only the "low" mood pole.

- **Signs excessive spending may be linked to depression:**

  o Regret or guilt follows purchases

  o Spending beyond means, often secretly

o Using shopping to feel "something" or to escape emotional pain

o A pattern of spending spikes during periods of sadness, loneliness, or stress.

The ability to hide depression can make it harder for others to recognize when help is truly needed. It takes discernment and observation or knowledge of "signs" to recognize when someone is masking depression.

Finding Hope Again

Healing from the depression stage of grief requires intentional steps, even when it feels impossible. Here are some ways to begin finding hope again:

- **Acknowledge the Pain:** Stop pretending. Give yourself permission to grieve.

- **Seek Support:** Open up to a trusted friend, family member, pastor, or counselor.

- **Develop Healthy Coping Mechanisms:** Replace destructive habits with activities that promote healing, such as journaling, exercise, or creative outlets.

- **Accountability Person:** Someone that will observe and inform or make aware of unhealthy behavior or activities.

- **Reconnect Spiritually:** Lean into prayer, worship, and God's promises of healing and restoration.

- **Allow Yourself to Feel:** Numbing the pain prolongs it; allowing yourself to process emotions leads to true healing.

- **Intentionality:** Be intentional about creating healthy habits such as exercise, reading, connecting with others and even joining a community that serves as a support group.

Emerging from the Darkness

Depression can feel like an inescapable pit, but the truth is that healing is possible. It does not happen overnight, and it does not mean the pain disappears completely. But step by step, light begins to break through the darkness. The memories remain, but the weight of grief becomes easier to carry.

Prayer to Overcome Depression in Grief

Merciful Father,

I ask You now, Father, to break the chains of hopelessness that have gripped my heart. Breathe life into places that feel dead. Replace despair with hope, mourning with comfort, and heaviness with Your garment of praise. Strengthen me when I cannot stand on my own and remind me daily that Your mercies are new every morning.

When I am tempted to isolate myself or believe that joy is out of reach, whisper Your truth to my soul. Remind me that You have plans for my future—plans to give me hope, a future and an expected end and not harm. Fill me with the peace that surpasses understanding and help me to trust that healing is possible, even now.

Jesus, You were a man of sorrows and acquainted with grief. You understand my pain intimately. Holy Spirit, be my Comforter, and let Your comfort surround me like a shield. Jesus be my Good Sheperd and guide me to still waters for the restoration of my soul.

Today, I am choosing to reject every lie that tells me I'll always feel this way and be in this situation. I speak life and joy over my soul, and I choose to receive Your healing and cling to Your promises. In the name of Jesus Christ, Amen.

Move Forward

Moving forward from depression involves consciously integrating these healthy coping strategies—seeking professional help, staying connected, maintaining self-care routines, engaging in meaningful practices such as prayer and meditation on the word, and setting manageable goals. While depression may persist, embracing these steps helps gradually shift towards emotional healing and prepares the heart for the upward turn. It's important to remember that grief doesn't necessarily follow a fixed sequence; depression may overlap with other stages or occur in isolation. Regardless of how your personal journey unfolds, intentional engagement with your emotions and support systems will ultimately lead to healing and renewed hope.

If you find yourself stuck in this stage, know that you are not alone. Your grief is valid, but it does not have to define your future. There is hope, even when you cannot see it.

In the next chapter, we will explore the next stage of grief—**the upward turn**—where the journey shifts from depression to realizing the possibility of living again.

CHAPTER SEVEN

The Upward Turn — Moving From Pain To Renewal

Grief, when fully experienced, is a journey with many valleys, and for a long time, it can feel like there is no way out. The darkness, the weight, and the sorrow seem endless. But there comes a point, sometimes unexpectedly, when a shift begins to take place—a small glimmer of light breaking through the heaviness. This stage of grief is known as the **upward turn**—a transition from deep sorrow into renewal. It does not mean the pain of loss disappears, nor does it mean forgetting what has happened, but it does mean that life begins to feel possible again.

The upward turn is the stage where healing starts to take root. It is the point at which the intensity of grief lessens, and moments of peace begin to emerge. The unbearable weight of emotions starts to lift, and though sadness may still linger, it no longer consumes every thought. While the tears still fall, you can finish your sentence without getting chocked up or continue your day without falling into a deep state of paralyzing sorrow.

What the Upward Turn Looks Like

The upward turn is not a single moment, but rather a series of small shifts. It can look different for each person, but common signs of entering this stage include:

- **Less Emotional Turmoil** — The extreme waves of sorrow, anger, and guilt begin to subside, and emotions become more manageable.

- **Increased Energy and Motivation** - Simple daily tasks no longer feel as exhausting, and there is a willingness to engage with life again.

- **Renewed Interest in Activities** - Hobbies, social interactions, and passions that once felt meaningless start to bring enjoyment again.

- **New Perspectives on Loss** - A deeper understanding that loss does not erase love, and that honoring what was lost does not mean staying in perpetual grief.

- **Hope for the Future** - A growing belief that joy, purpose, and fulfillment can still be found beyond the pain.

For some, the upward turn happens gradually over time. For others, it may be triggered by a defining moment—an event such as a marriage or newborn baby, a promotion, a court case won, a realization, or a spiritual awakening like inner healing that leads to freedom.

People Experience Upward Turn Differently

While the upward turn signals a shift in grief, how people reach this stage varies widely based on their experiences, beliefs, and support systems. Here are a few ways people have navigated their journey toward renewal:

1. Finding Purpose Through Service

Some people find healing in helping others. Volunteering, mentoring, or starting a cause related to their loss can provide a sense of purpose. By serving others, grief transforms from a weight that cripples to a force that fuels transformation in the lives of others.

2. Strengthening Faith and Spiritual Growth

For many, the upward turn comes through a deepening of faith.

Turning to God for comfort, leaning into prayer, and seeking godly guidance can create a renewed sense of peace and trust in a greater purpose. Faith does not erase grief, but it provides a foundation for hope beyond loss.

3. Rebuilding Through Creativity and Expression

Creative outlets have helped many people process their emotions and move toward healing; building, arts/crafts, writing, music, painting, or storytelling can turn pain into something beautiful.

Creativity offers a way to express what words cannot always capture, allowing emotions to be released in a healing way.

4. Embracing Personal Growth and Change

Sometimes, the upward turn leads to transformation. People find themselves making significant life changes, whether through new careers, new locations, or newfound passions.

The pain of loss can be the catalyst for a new chapter—one shaped by resilience and newfound purpose.

My Personal Experience

For years, I never thought I would reach this stage. Depression held me captive, and my grief felt like a prison. But when I gave my life to Jesus at 22, something shifted. It was not an instant fix, nor did my pain disappear overnight, but I began to see a new path forward. The more I surrendered to the Lord, the more I allowed healing to take place.

I started making small changes—letting go of destructive habits, seeking healthier relationships, and embracing new opportunities. Where I once saw only pain, I began to see hope. It did not mean I forgot what I had lost, but I learned that healing did not mean erasing the past—it meant choosing to live beyond it.

The upward turn for me was realizing that my story was not over, that despite my grief, there was still purpose in my life, still joy to be found, and still love to give and receive.

Steps Toward the Upward Turn

If you are still in the depths of grief, know that the upward turn is possible. Here are some steps to help move in that direction:

1. **Allow Yourself to Heal -** Give yourself permission to experience joy again without guilt.

2. **Surround Yourself with Support -** Whether through friends, faith, counseling, or community; do not grieve alone, do not isolate!

3. **Find Purpose in the Pain -** Look for ways to honor what was lost while embracing what remains.

4. **Take Small Steps -** Healing is not immediate; even small acts of self-care and reflection are progress.

5. **Trust That It Gets Better -** The pain may never fully disappear, but it will not always feel this heavy.

6. **Meditate on the Word of God -** There is a comfort found in none other than Jesus and His Word brings healing like no other.

Prayer of Thanksgiving for the Upward Turn

Abba Father,

Daddy God, I thank You, from the depths of my heart, I thank You—for holding me and being the glory and the lifter up of my head. You have been faithful through my tears, patient through my questions, and present through my pain. Now, as I feel the shift—this upward turn in my journey of grief—I pause to say, thank You.

Thank You for not letting grief define me, but for using it to refine me. Thank You for the strength to rise again, even when I thought I never would. Thank You for surrounding me with new mercies each morning and for pouring hope into my heart when I felt empty. It was You who carried me as nothing else would do.

Lord, I sense Your healing at work in my heart, though the sorrow is still real, so is the joy that is returning to my soul. I embrace this moment with gratitude and reverence, knowing that every upward step is a sign of Your restoring power. You are rebuilding the broken places and repairing the breach and I trust You to complete the good work You began in me.

As I continue forward, I ask for courage; courage to keep choosing life, love, and You. Help me not walk in fear, or a state of paranoia wondering what else I will lose. Let my testimony of Your faithfulness be a light for others still in the valley. Let joy arise in me like the dawn and peace be my portion.

Daddy God, thank You for being my Rock, my Redeemer, and the Anchor of my soul. I love You, and I trust You with the rest of my journey. In Jesus' name, Amen.

Moving Forward

The upward turn is not the end of grief but the beginning of a new direction in the healing process. It is the point where loss no longer defines every moment, where love for what was lost coexists with hope for the future. If you are in this stage, embrace it. Allow yourself to move forward, rejecting feelings of guilt because you are advancing on your journey toward healing. Remember, healing is not a betrayal of what was lost—it is an acknowledgment that life is still worth living.

In the next chapter, we will explore **reconstruction and rebuilding,** where grief transforms into action, and new possibilities begin to take shape. Keep in mind that grief doesn't necessarily happen in this order or all at one time or even at all, and that is perfectly okay. Each journey is uniquely personal.

CHAPTER EIGHT

Reconstruction And Rebuilding

Celebrate this moment—you've come so far! Reaching reconstruction and rebuilding is a significant achievement on your journey through grief. This stage signals that grief, though deeply felt, no longer governs your every moment. Instead, your experiences become powerful motivators for change and growth. It is here, in this remarkable phase, where sorrow transforms into purposeful action, where heartache becomes strength, and where the path forward is reshaped by new possibilities and renewed hope. Embrace this powerful turning point, knowing that life, although forever altered, is now ripe with opportunities for meaningful reconstruction and renewal.

Reconstruction is about learning how to live again. It is where the fresh wind of renewal propels us forward, not because we forget what we lost, but because we learn to build upon it. This stage involves actively making choices to restore what was broken, create something new, and step into a future that holds meaning beyond grief.

What Reconstruction and Rebuilding Look Like

Rebuilding after loss is not about returning to what was but about constructing a life that embraces renewal and aligns with your new normal. This stage looks different for each person and it takes on unique forms such as:

- **Embracing New Roles -** such as matriculating into higher education, reentry into workforce, changing careers, engaging in community service projects or advocacy.

- **Pursuing Dreams That Were Once on Hold -** Someone who abandoned their passions due to grief reigniting their creative pursuits.

- **Deepening Relationships -** Choosing to nurture new and existing relationships.

- **Creating a Legacy in Honor of a Loved One -** Establishing charities, scholarships, or projects that reflect the values of the person lost.

- **Prioritizing Health and Self-Care** — Making choices to heal physically, emotionally, and spiritually.

- **Exploring Faith in a Deeper Way -** Strengthening your relationship with God and allowing Him to direct your steps while gaining a new perspective on life's purpose.

- **Making Environmental Changes** — Moving to a new home, redecorating, or removing items that keep you emotionally tied to the past.

Reconstruction is not an overnight process; however, it is intentional, deliberate, and often requires stepping outside of your comfort zone.

Moving or Removing Items

For many, their environment carries emotional weight, filled with reminders of what was lost. While some find comfort in keeping everything the same, others discover that changing their surroundings allows them to step into a new season of healing.

- **Moving to a New Home:** Relocating can symbolize a fresh start, an opportunity to create new memories unburdened by constant reminders of loss. Some people move to escape the pain, while others move because they recognize that their healing requires a different setting.

- **Rearranging or Redecorating a Space:** Some find peace in changing their living environment—repainting walls, redecorating rooms, or redesigning spaces to reflect their new season of life.

- **Removing Items That Hold Painful Memories:** Letting go of personal belongings that keep one tied to grief can be a freeing step. This does not mean discarding everything, but rather, thoughtfully choosing what to keep and what no longer serves emotional well-being - it could prove to be beneficial to allow someone to assist you in this process as others may be able to identify unhealthy attachments that you are not able to readily identify.

Moving on does not mean forgetting. It means allowing oneself to step into something new while honoring what remains in the heart.

Examples of Rebuilding After Grief

The stories of those who have reached this stage are inspiring because they remind us that healing does not mean forgetting—it means choosing to live fully despite the pain of loss.

1. A Father Who Lost His Son to Violence

After his teenage son was killed in a senseless act of violence, a father could have remained in bitterness and despair. Instead, he turned his grief into advocacy. He founded a youth mentorship program in his community, working with at-risk teens to prevent the same fate his son endured. His pain became his purpose, and he transformed his grief into a mission that changed lives.

2. A Woman Who Found Love Again After Losing Her Spouse

For years after her husband's death, she believed she could never love again. The grief felt too deep, the memories too strong. But as healing took root, she opened her heart once more. Rebuilding for her meant understanding that love was not meant to replace what was lost but to expand her capacity to cherish life anew. She remarried—not as a replacement, but as a continuation of love's journey.

This also applies to pets as some may deny themselves the enjoyment of owning another pet due to the painful loss of a previous fur-baby.

3. A Young Adult Who Overcame Addiction After Losing a Parent

Devastated by the sudden death of his mother, a young man spiraled into substance abuse to cope. For years, he remained stuck in self-destruction until he made the choice to rebuild. Fie sought help, embraced faith, and eventually became a counselor, using his own experiences to guide others toward healing.

4. A Grieving Mother Who Became an Advocate

After losing her daughter to illness, a mother struggled with the void left behind. Instead of allowing grief to consume her, she started a nonprofit dedicated to funding medical research and supporting families facing similar battles. Her daughter's memory lived on through every life the foundation helped.

My Personal Experience

The choice to rebuild did not come easily; it required me to break free from the comfort of pain and step into the unknown.

My reconstruction began when I gave my life to Jesus and allowed Him to redefine my story. I let go of self-destructive habits, walked away from toxic relationships, and embraced a new identity—one rooted in healing, faith, and purpose. The process was not instant, but each decision to move forward led me to a place of restoration I never imagined was possible.

Rebuilding meant choosing to live again, not just merely existing. It meant using my pain to fuel something greater—helping others who are walking the same path, showing them that grief does not have to be the end. It meant stepping into my calling and allowing my story to be a testimony of transformation. Do I still think about them? Yes. Do I feel sadden by their absence? Yes. But I don't linger in the past as I have learned to enjoy the memories without living with the guilt of moving on.

Steps to Begin Reconstruction

If you find yourself at this stage, ready to rebuild but unsure how, here are some ways to start:

1. **Define What Rebuilding Means for You -** Healing looks different for everyone; identify what moving forward means in your personal journey. It could be a small step such as giving away the toys, clothes and things that you cannot use but others may benefit from, washing the clothes that carry the scent of that person because it brings you back to an exact time, place or memory, or it could be as grand as selling the home you purchased together because every area of it is filled with memories that keep you in perpetual moments of sorrow.

2. **Set Small, Achievable Goals -** Start with small changes, whether it's reconnecting with others, pursuing a passion, or simply practicing self-care.

3. **Surround Yourself with Encouragement -** Stay connected to people who uplift you, whether through faith, friendship, or mentorship.

4. **Honor the Past While Embracing the Future -** Moving forward does not mean leaving behind memories but allowing them to inspire you.

5. **Trust That You Are Not Alone -** God walks with you in this process; lean into Him for guidance and strength.

Living Beyond Grief

Reconstruction and rebuilding does not mean grief disappears. Instead, they mean that the emotions that come from grief has transformed into something that no longer holds you captive.

If you are in this stage, embrace it. Let the fresh wind of renewal carry you forward. Know that the pain you have endured is not wasted—it is the very thing that is shaping you into someone stronger, wiser, and more compassionate than before and equipped to help others through the valley you emerged out of.

In the next chapter, we will explore **acceptance** and finding meaning, the final stage of grief, where peace and purpose come together to create a life that honors both the loss and the future that awaits.

CHAPTER NINE

Acceptance: Finding Meaning — The Final Stage Of Grief

Acceptance is often misunderstood as the absence of grief, but in reality, it is the integration of grief into a new way of living. It is not about forgetting, nor does it mean that pain is completely gone. Instead, acceptance is the place where grief and peace coexist, where sorrow no longer defines every moment, and where meaning begins to emerge from the experience of loss.

This stage is about living again—not as though loss never happened, but in a way that honors both the past and the future. It is about recognizing that grief has changed you, yet you are still capable of joy, love, and purpose.

What Acceptance Looks Like

Acceptance does not come with a dramatic moment of realization; rather, it unfolds gradually. It can look different for each person, but some common signs include:

- **The Ability to Talk About the Loss Without Returning to Stage** 1 — Memories are no longer triggers that keep you in cycles of prolonged and debilitating sorrow, but instead moments that bring reflection and appreciation.

- **Crying Without Being Consumed by Pain -** Tears may still fall, but they do not pull you back into cycles of despair and depression.

- **Feeling Gratitude for the Time Shared -** Focusing more on the impact the lost loved one had on your life rather than just how empty yours is because of their absence.

- **Learning to Laugh Again** — Laughter returns when thinking of the memories and moments you shared with those that you loss.

- **Celebrating the Contributions of Those Who Passed -** Honoring their influence in positive ways, whether through storytelling, traditions, or acts of service.

- **Finding Purpose Beyond Grief -** Discovering ways to live fully again while carrying the love and memories of what was lost.

For some, acceptance happens sooner than expected. For others, it takes years. But the key element of this stage is that grief no longer controls every aspect of life. The memories remain, and the pain no longer has the power to define the future.

How Different People Reach Acceptance

Reaching acceptance is a deeply personal journey. Here are some ways people have arrived at this stage:

1. Spiritual Growth Through Prayer and Worship: Many Christians find solace in prayer and worship, allowing their relationship with God to bring comfort and healing.

- A woman who lost her spouse started waking up early each morning to spend time in worship, using praise as a way to combat sorrow.

- A grieving father began journaling his prayers, pouring out his emotions to God and finding peace in surrendering his pain to the Lord.

- Someone who struggled with anger toward God after their loss eventually found healing by meditating on Psalms and allowing Scripture to restore their trust in Him.

2. Studying the Bible for Strength and Guidance

God's Word offers reassurance, hope, and the reminder that grief is not the end of the story.

- A man grieving the loss of his mother found comfort in studying the book of Job, realizing that suffering is temporary, and God's restoration is always possible.

- A widow who felt abandoned found strength in Isaiah 41:10, holding onto God's promise that He was with her and that He would uphold her.

- A family who lost everything in a crisis turned to Romans 8:28, trusting that God could bring good out of their loss.

3. Serving Others as a Form of Healing

Jesus taught that serving others brings fulfillment, and many who have reached acceptance find purpose in giving back.

- A man who lost his child began volunteering at his church's children's ministry, turning his grief into an opportunity to bless other children.

- A woman who lost her husband started a support group for widows, creating a space where others could heal together through faith.

- A former addict who lost loved ones to substance abuse became a mentor, using his testimony to help others break free from addiction through Christ.

4. Trusting God's Plan and Finding New Purpose

Even when loss is devastating, God can bring something new out of it.

- A young woman who lost her father felt directionless until she began seeking God's will, leading her to a calling in ministry.

- A man who lost his business due to grief realized that God was redirecting him to something greater, leading him to start a nonprofit that helped others rebuild their lives.

- A grieving mother, who once questioned her faith, later found herself deepening her relationship with God, discovering a renewed sense of purpose through leading Bible studies.

My Personal Experience

Reaching acceptance for me was about "moving on" in life free of guilt, remorse, pain and depression. There was a time when even mentioning their names would send me spiraling back to stage one, drowning in sorrow as if the loss had just occurred.

But then something changed. I reached a place where I could talk about them, honor their memory, and reflect on the impact they had on my life—without falling back into depression or cycles of pain. I could shed tears, but those tears were no longer a sign of despair; they reflected love.

Instead of just mourning their absence, I learned to celebrate the ways they shaped me, the lessons they taught me, and the love they left behind. Their presence in my life was a gift, and instead of focusing solely on the void, I began focusing on the blessings they had given me.

This was acceptance for me: remembering without being destroyed, honoring without being trapped in sorrow, and living in a way that made their love and impact meaningful.

Living a Life That Honors Both the Loss and the Future

Acceptance is about moving forward in a way that allows life to flourish again. It is about finding peace, embracing joy, and stepping into a future that is not dictated by pain.

If you have reached this stage, celebrate it. If you are still on the journey, trust that it is possible. This is the final stage of grief, but it is also the beginning of something new: a life that honors both what was lost and the future that awaits.

CHAPTER TEN

A Prayer For Those Grieving

Heavenly Father,

You said you are close to the brokenhearted and you save those who are crushed in spirit, right now Lord, I am hurting, and my heart is broken. My desire if for You to take this pain away. My mind wishes I could go back in time to prevent this from happening, but I recognize that no matter how much I desire this, there is nothing that can change what has occurred. So, I ask You to help and strengthen me through this process. Help me not to self-medicate, help me not to compensate for my loss in unhealthy ways, help me not to wallow in self-pity or isolate myself.

Lord, I do not pretend to understand all or even any of this, nor do I know why it happened to me; so help me not to dwell on why it happened but help me to trust in You with all my heart and lean not unto my own understanding. Strengthen me so that I do not remain in any stage of grief longer than I should. Give me the courage to move forward while leaning on your as my Comforter and Strengthener. Help me not to divert my focus to avoid feeling the pain of loss, but to walk through this valley with You by my side. Help me to feel the pain without becoming a prisoner to it. Help me to remember that my loss is not an indication that my life has ended, but rather that this closed chapter is the birthing of a new beginning. Help me to see and perceive the new things that you are doing in my life.

Help me to hold on to memories without slipping into depression. Help me to remember past experiences without being trapped in them. Strengthen me to fill the void and empty spaces with You and You along for my flesh and my heart may fail, but You are the strength of my heart and my portion forever.

Today I am choosing not to allow grief to overtake me, and I choose not to partner with fear; for you have given me power, love and a sound mind. In the day when I called, You answered me; and You strengthened me with strength in my inner self. I call upon you today for strength over fear and depression and a lying spirit that says this is my new norm. I am choosing today not to make a monument of my pain but to create a movement to help others through theirs. You have given me everything pertaining to life and godliness and You have empowered to resist partnership with self-pity or avoidance of pain.

Today Father, I choose to let go of all those that I have loss to death, or broken relationships and friendships that I held on to for so long in an unhealthy manner and I release them and the associated pain, anger, sorrow and sadness that are tied to their absence in my life that have lingered in my emotions for far too long. I command all grief, pain, anger, sorrow and sadness to leave me now; I command you to leave my thoughts, emotions, mind and body and I receive Jesus's healing, peace and joy in exchange. I receive a garment of praise in exchange for the spirit of heaviness and I yoke myself to You Lord Jesus and choose to learn of You, for You are meek and lowly in heart so that I may And rest for my soul.

I praise You Lord, because you are the Father of compassion and the God of all comfort, who comforts me in all my troubles, so that I can comfort those in any trouble with the comfort I myself receive from You. Thank you Lord, for the time I had with, I cherish every moment and look forward to what you have in store for me. In Jesus' name, Amen.

CHAPTER ELEVEN

Supporting Someone Who Is Grieving

Over the course of my life, from losing my loved ones to body parts, I have learned that well-meaning people do not know how to navigate grief and tend to say things that annoy, irritate or even anger the grieving person.

TIPS FOR CAREGIVERS OF THE GRIEVING

What Not to Say to Someone Grieving:

- "I know exactly how you feel." - Because you really don't.
- "The same thing happened to me and I..." It's not about you.
- "Everything happens for a reason." - Insensitive.
- "They're in a better place." - We don't know you.
- "God needed them more than we did" - His Will to be done on Earth "through us" ...
- "At least they're no longer suffering." - True, but the grieving person is and your statement added to that pain.
- "You need to move on." - Insensitive.
- "Time heals all wounds." — Time heals nothing.
- "God never gives you more than you can handle." Insensitive.
- "You need to stay strong for others." - This takes away their right to mourn.

What You Should Say:

- "I'm here for you whenever you need me." (and mean it!)
- "I can't imagine how difficult this must be for you."
- "Would you like to talk about it, or would you prefer some company?"
- "How can I best support you right now?"

What you Should Offer:

- Offer meals of person that's grieving choice
- Clean their home
- Watch their children
- Quietly sit with them
- Embrace them
- Run errands or tend to any task that have gone unattended.
- Listen actively and compassionately, without giving unsolicited advice or judgment.
- Provide ongoing support—grief doesn't have a timeline, and ongoing care can be invaluable.
- Send text messages letting them know you are thinking of them.

The most important thing you can do to aid a person that is grieving is to be consistent! So often the "I am here for you" starts to diminish around the 1st week after the funeral, or surgery or loss and those that "committed" to the cause have gone on with their lives forgetting the person they committed to serve during their time of loss - don't be that person! The most selfless thing you can do is make it your personal mission to be one of the many people who assist with the healing journey.

ABOUT THE AUTHOR

Rhonda is a wife, mother, Board Certified Christian Counselor, and Chaplain whose personal experiences and post graduate education powerfully equip her to counsel others through trauma, grief, anger, depression, and anxiety. Her life stands as a testament to the unwavering goodness of God amid adversity, as she has navigated profound loss throughout her life, including the passing of parents, grandparents, siblings, a child, significant others, beloved pets, inheritance, property and double mastectomy due to cancer. Post salvation she relied on the grace and mercy of an Almighty God, to guide her through the dark nights of the soul, revealing that life can indeed continue after loss.

To schedule a consultation for grief, acute trauma, depression, or anger email rhonda@eycounseling.org

www.ingramcontent.com/pod-product-compliance
Lightning Source LLC
Chambersburg PA
CBHW061710120626
46550CB00003B/1174